From Darkness to Light

Angela French

Presentation by *BookLeaf Publishing*

Web: www.bookleafpub.com

E-mail: info@bookleafpub.com

ISBN: 9789357691918

First edition 2023

DEDICATION

I wish to dedicate this book to my Uncle John. I was 14 when he died, and that was when I wrote my first ever poem, through grief. Always loved. Always missed.

ACKNOWLEDGEMENT

To my Mum and Dad, who always believe in me, and even named me quite poetically. My sisters, who gave me quiet inspiration when we were young. My husband and children, who have always got my back (and to add - my daughters, who are quite the little poets themselves!) To William Wordsworth, who started my love of poetry. And to everyone near and dear to me, those I love/have loved and lost. You have all pulled something poetic from my heart. I thank you all x

Angela Dawn Rose French

PREFACE

A lot of my writing came through grief and painful life experiences. Then the book started to look a bit depressing, so I threw in a couple of light-hearted poems to lift the mood!

 These others are from various times of joy and light in my life, and there have been many more - luckily so much more to outweigh the dark times now, but I choose to share most of the poems that I thought could help or relate to others who may be struggling.

 Grief, pain and dark times come in many forms. My experiences, and the experiences of those close to me, are personal to us, and do not necessarily speak for others. Everyone experiences things in their own personal way.

 I hope that if you have taken the time to read through these poems, you find one that touches your heart or gives you some comfort. Or you may simply find one that is relatable.

 If you are experiencing any grief, or dark/painful times, find some courage and please do find someone to share it with. Do not suffer alone. You will find a way through.

John

The man who was always there for me
The man in all my dreams
The man who comforted me when I cried
Or when something bursts inside...and screams.

Never had I really shown
How much I loved this man
I never had the chance to say goodbye.
Now he's in another land

He is in a land of freedom
Where all the spirits roam
They do not suffer any pain
In the place that they call home

This man is always with me
His spirit is never gone
The man of the past... and presence!
My loving Uncle John

Wave of grief

Today I had a moment
where something made me smile
And I thought about how you'd react
At this moment.... for a while

I thought about the things you'd say
And all the things you'd do
And then suddenly I'd remember
That you left us far too soon

It made me feel quite sad at first
That I didn't have you there
To talk about the thing I'd seen
To laugh and joke and share

My throat swelled up, I choked back tears
I was angry, I was blue...
But then I smiled... because this thing
Reminded me of you…

Hero

Our hero, standing tall. A pillar of strength, like a lighthouse, steadfast, unafraid of the storms around him. The winds may batter and blow, but he stands unaffected and bold. A beacon of light shining brightly in the darkness, keeping his beloved fleet safe from the rough seas. He is a courageous tower above the rocks of despair, mildly weathered over time yet never losing his decorum, dignity, and magnificence.

Each day he basks in the glorious sun, keeping a watchful eye on his legacy below, watching his fleet grow and find glory. Drinking in his prosperity. At night he stands brave within the darkness, watching and protecting. Too soon the nights become longer, and the light dims. The days in the sun and the joy of his fleet have fulfilled him. It's time to rest among the stars, keeping his watchful eye on another light. It's time for the fleet to come in.

We are now the pillar of strength. The light shines as brightly as it did before, through his fleet's love and unity. We will forever be under his beacon of light, we will follow his star and be guided by him. Our tower of strength. Our Dad.

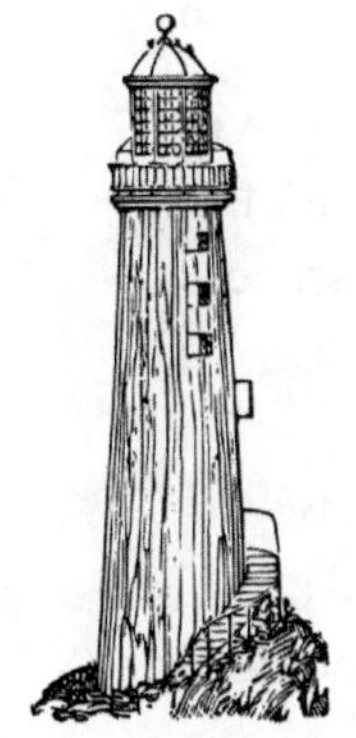

Evil never wins

A dark shadow of Evil
A wicked torment of fate
An imp in the darkness
That Satan creates

Stealing my purity
Soothing the bad
Taking all the courage
That I ever had

I'm left walking with sinners
Wandering baron lands
He took all my freedom
Away by the hand

Impossible to forget
I cannot let go
I want to shout to the world
But I want nobody to know

I'm left all alone
In an endless dark world
Wondering what will become
Of such a broken girl

It's time to rise up
Take hold of my mind
I won't let it defeat me
This is my time

Changing my future
Forgetting my past
No longer in my life
A shadow he will cast

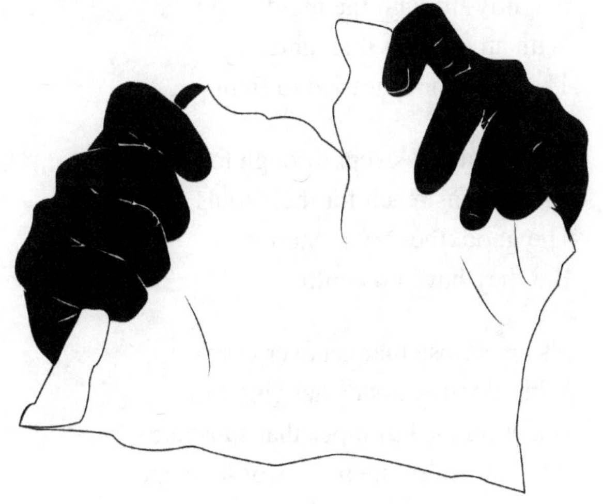

Black Dreams

I remember long ago
When the Sun did shine
And all my happy memories
Stretched out in a flawless line

In the darkness, Stars were shining
Brightly through the night
With an eerie Evil laughter
That the innocent tried to fight

Sweet Angels swept through torture
As Demons reach for their souls
The good, they try to stop it
But they have no control

It's an eclipse that is never over
With gloomy clouds hanging low
But at times, I glimpse that sunshine
Bringing sweet memories of long ago

Missing you

Wandering alone, I glance upon
The roaring, great dark Sea
A teardrop shows I'm wishing you
Were by my side with me

I take a lonely walk along
The glistening, cool wet sand
I close my eyes and think of you
Wishing I could hold your hand

The sky above is threatening
The mild air turns to cold
My loving heart can't beat the same
When you're not here for me to hold

I'll take this lonely path each day
Through Sun, Wind, and Rain
Remembering you and longing for
The day we are together again

Busker

On this warm and sunny afternoon
I watch the world go by
Listening to the soft sweet music
Playing by the riverside

Floating on that Summer breeze
The tunes drift through my window
Around my head, they dance and tease
And fill my room with a musical glow

I gaze upon the passing crowd
Who do not seem to hear
These wondrous tunes he plays for them
Which fills my heart with cheer

He plays out all my favourite songs
That makes me smile with glee
And though he does not know I'm here
Please play another song for me

Rhiannon

The sky above grows still and dark
The gentle wind turns cold
Our hearts are feeling empty now
That we don't have you here to hold

We thank you for the times we shared
And the Joy we felt together
The little time we had you there
Will stay with us forever

Our love for you is deeper
Than any Ocean blue
And we want you to remember
That we are missing you

You leave us now to join the stars
It's time for us to part
We briefly held you in our arms
But we will forever hold you in our hearts

Rainbow Baby

The wind has blown the leaves away
The trees have lost their charm
But I have springtime every day
Now I have you in my arms

When rainy days dampen smiles
Whilst the sun is struggling through
The low mood only lasts a while
As I laugh and play with you

The nights are dark and turning cold
And Snow is on the ground
But in my heart, it's warmth I hold
As I watch you sleeping safe and sound

With all your colours I can see
Through rain or wind or snow
You are my beautiful Baby
You are my true Rainbow

Losing ourselves

As we age, we lose ourselves
That free spirit we had as a child
The carefree wonders and mighty dreams
Our running so free and wild

Then the fiery rebellious teenage years
With headstrong ideas and ways
Replaced with a longing to be older
Wishing away our youthful days

We have our fun and then we grow
A family? two kids, maybe three?
We change our views to suit others
Losing sight of our identity

Then time ticks on and we panic
"Have I really lost sight of 'me'?
Is it too late to get me back?
Surely it cannot be..."

We make changes to be who we once were
Some accuse that "you have changed!"
As others simply cannot see
"I was always this way... I just 'aged'.."

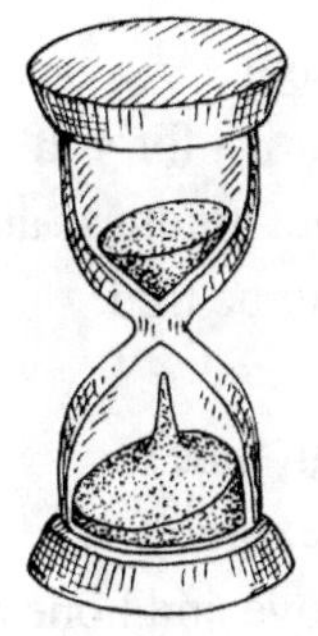

A Mother's thoughts

Am I doing enough
to shape your worlds for you
to teach you about kindness and values
to be good, and to be true

Do I offer enough time?
and help you to explore?
Do I show you love and honesty?
Are you ever left wanting more?

Am I loving and kind?
Am I the best that I can be?
Do I make you feel safe and loved?
Do I treat you all equally?

Please know that I love you
the best that I know how
you fill my heart with so much joy
each one of you, still now

Loving you is easy
each with your own quirky ways
you are my proudest moments
and my happiest of days

Impossible to put into words
how motherhood has felt
I couldn't feel any happier
over the hand that I've been dealt

I hope that I have done enough
and I've been a good mum to you
whatever may come our way
I will always be here for you

Through every celebration or every storm
feeling happy, or feeling glum
you need not ever feel alone,
for you will always have your Mum

The Dark Place

At times it feels that the darkness
Consumes me, and holds me back
However, I try to move forward
The shadows appear to attack

It's lonely in the dark place
But my smile can hide it well
Nobody seems to care or see
the reality, so I don't tell

What is the point of my being?
I ask myself most days
I'm just in pain and living in shadows
I'm useless, I just get in the way

I can't get out of the dark place
I just want to be happy and free
Apparently, there are people who love me
If that's true, then why can't they see?

I feel so lonely and helpless
Some days I'm in utter despair
A part of me wants to reach out
But rejection is too hard to bear

I want to try, should I go and seek
Some help from someone I know?
Or from a stranger who doesn't know me
If it fails, then I can let go….

I'm told the pain won't last forever
They're foolish to think this is true
But I can talk so freely and openly
I'm not judged…. this is something new…

The dark place still surrounds me
And most days I'm still in such pain
But this person who doesn't know me
Is bringing some light to my life again

I've spent so long in the dark place
It's been just me for so long
But today, I shared it with a loved one
And now together with them, I feel strong

The pain, it won't last forever
Call me foolish if you will
But I have lived through the dark place
And some days, I live it still

The dark place no longer consumes me
I share it often, without fear
It all began with a stranger
And my courage, and look, I'm still here

The pain really won't last forever
Find courage, try not to doubt
Find light in the simplest of places
And most importantly – talk it out.

It's OK to cry

I can see you hide the tears that fall
and that pain you try to fight
The mottled sky that surrounds us all
holds another precious star tonight

The tears, they soon begin to fade
but the anger remains inside
you feel you have to close it in
put on a front...that manly pride

You feel as though you are alone
with your days, so empty and sad
and your heartbreak when you remember
even the good times that you had

You struggle to show your emotions
you say "It makes me a weaker man"
But strength can lie in confronting your fears
and with my help, I know you can

So when you feel you want to cry
and you can't control the pain
Don't try to hide it all away
You can show those tears to me again

The Great Man

The Man who won a thousand hearts
Sleeps peacefully today
Though, truly we could never part
As in our hearts, he'll stay

Never could we forget his smile
His laughter, and his love
remembering his warm embrace
That now shines down from above

He really was the greatest man
His legacy lives on
In each and every one of us
He never really could be gone

Our hearts are feeling heavy
The tears fall from our eyes
But through it, we find comfort
Knowing that true love never dies

The man who won a thousand hearts
Sleeps peacefully today
To us, he was the greatest man
Perfect in every way

I have a Voice

I have a Voice
That should be heard
Though it's not very loud
I've tried my best
I've made mistakes
It's hard to make you proud

I have a Voice
Though it's quite small
I'm trying to make it louder
I have ideas
I should be heard
At last, I feel empowered

I have a Voice
Don't shut me up
Don't silence me this way
Teach me to speak
Not 'do as you do'
I am valid, I've things to say!

I have a Voice
I have my dreams
That I know I can achieve
I am stronger

I am confident
I won't let this new voice leave

This is my voice
It's louder now
I've really learned a lot
I'm brave and free
So just remember
It's the quiet ones you have to watch!

My first loves

My first loves, my whole world,
The constants in my life
The ones who have never judged me
Who are there for me day and night

I've indescribable love for them
They've given me a lifetime of joy
They're responsible for all my values,
That I've passed to my own girls and boys

I'm sure that they've never seen themselves
As perfect, though it is true
To me, they are both just that
Simply faultless, through and through

They'd never know it fully
But they saved me in so many ways
They pulled me out of dark times,
And offered me brighter days

Every decision I've made in life
They've always been on my side
They're the first ones that I think of
And my thoughts hold nothing but pride

I'm truly blessed to know such love
And the sacrifices made for me
All for the sake of my happiness
And that of my family

They're the first ones that I long for
Whenever I'm happy or sad
My first loves, my whole world
My wonderful Mum and Dad

It's okay to heal

It's okay to be happy
To laugh and smile again
And add some light into our days
To balance out the pain

Our grief, it never leaves us
Our lives just grow around it now
We'll never forget our loved ones,
We'll find a way through somehow

Our loved ones, they'd be happy
To see us doing well.
We will feel some joy again
Let's be patient - time will tell.

Taking small steps forwards
Doesn't mean we'll miss them less.
We can get through this pain,
And we can only do our best

It's okay to feel happy
It's okay to heal the pain
We'll find ourselves a new normal,
Until we meet our loved ones again

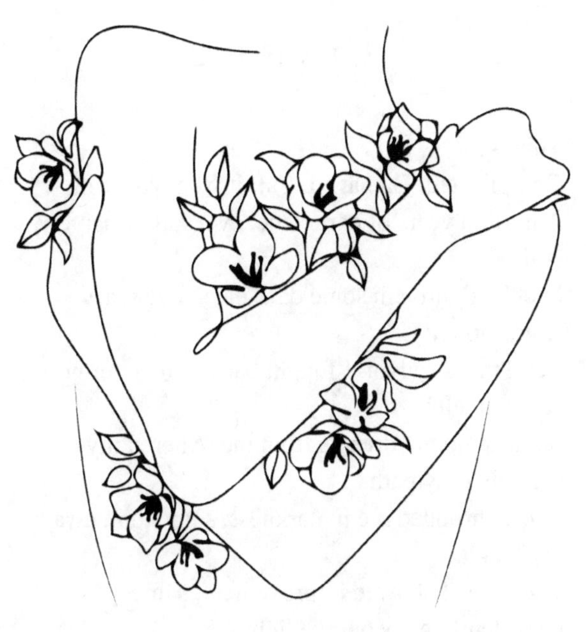

This is me

This is me
Complicated. Damaged. Call it what you will.
A million years of experience, yet full of naivety,
still.
I've lived through some dark days. I've scary
stories to tell.
Yet, I'm a survivor. I fought back. I'm better now,
can you tell?
Some stole my dreams from me. Altered my
smooth, easy path.
Some shrouded me in darkness, some took away
my laugh.
The times I showed improvement, some
persistently blew out the light.
Trampled on my confidence. Took away my fight.
But this is me.
I kept on going. Fought back. Ignored.
I focused on what, my life could have in store.
I will not let the past define who I am.
I control my destiny. I decide if I can.
I'm thankful in a way, for the pain some put me
through.
Yes. I give thanks to them. For showing me the
truth
For showing me I'm better. For helping me see,
Exactly what I don't want to be...
This is me.
I lived it. I suffered great pain.

I don't want to ever feel that again.
But I know now, that if I do,
I will survive it. I know this to be true.
Because this is me.
I work hard every day, to remember who I am.
All that I have worked for. My life. My path. My plan.
It's not easy. It never will be. But the work gets easier to handle
My confidence is stronger and the light remains bright on my candle.
This is me.
I'm not the first to come through these dark days.
I won't be the last, you will see a way.
If your dark times aren't over, just know that there's light.
You may not see it yet. But you must fight.
Look at me. A survivor. After all that I've been through.
This is me. This will be you.